Donald Berger

THE ROSE OF MAINE

SurVision Books

First published in 2024 by
SurVision Books
Dublin, Ireland
Reggio di Calabria, Italy
www.survisionmagazine.com

Copyright © Donald Berger, 2024

Cover image and design © SurVision Books, 2024

ISBN: 978-1-912963-52-2

This book is in copyright. No part of this publication may be reproduced, stored in a retrieval system, or transmitted in any form or by any means without the prior permission in writing from the publisher.

Acknowledgments

Grateful acknowledgment is made to the editors of the following, in which some of these poems, or versions of them, originally appeared:

The Alembic: "Elizabeth"
Alonsoville Voice: "False Memory"
Foundlings: "You"
The Nervous Breakdown: "Notifications"
New American Writing: "The Nice Woman Phones"
R&R: "Please"

CONTENTS

You	5
Stevie Wonder	6
Notifications	8
The Rose of Maine	10
I Was Trying	11
False Memory	14
Galatea	16
Central	18
Fried Eggs on Night	20
I'm Glad When You Rest	22
Please	23
Elizabeth	24
The Nice Woman Phones	25
Ruby Red	26
All the Sudden	28
Promising, New	30
Hamburger Theory	32
A Letter	34
"There was no way to tell..."	39

You

You as in what
Angle I saw you from

The birches, real ones,
Moved in a wild way
Past your shoulder

I knew then
What I can't think of
Every night
The room
Still has walls

And all of the ways
To do something
Work too hard

You that rushes in
Like a word

Is there more
Than sound
To the wind
Someone far off
Keeps asking

Stevie Wonder

This is the passage
my heart would play
if it were a harmonica

These are the shorts
and the shirt
I wouldn't wear

That is the window
to turn into
a different window

The beaches mimic a plateau
the music box a live concert
the desk a hall of colanders and bowls

The shoes that represent
my feet are literally suctioning
fear out of the floor

I'm unconscious
My subconscious
twists or pops whatever it finds

My mask
is the life mask
of a crash dummy that has smiled

The horns on my head
are made of hair
but they are still real horns

The cows that are feeding
on the grass high above
brush up against me as they pass

This is the passage
my heart is beating with
two beats to a measure

These are the fingers
that are nothing
but fingers

This the soft
the least deliberate attachment
of the tympanum

to its wave

Notifications

Jared Corner marked himself safe during Hurricane Matthew—South Carolina.
Jeffrey Presser Art shared Harried Devil's event with me: **Walter P. Cisco Prize (deadline Moon 1).**
Harriet Patricia Ciprio shared a link.
Mick Custer shared a link.
Kevin G. Destani invited me to his old page, **New Toes.**
Mia Hoskins shared **Snowcone Review's** photo.
Did I know David Pomegrant?
Did I know Jim Daily Heal?
Did I know Sheila Pounder-Crase?
Did I know Bob Jenerko?
Sammy Newton commented on her photo.
Did I know Shenai Preed?
Did I know Jana Income?
Nelly Lojack updated her status.
Jeb O'Broom added a new photo.
Hans Pleasureman invited me to like his page Remove.
Sallycaroline Thonkton shared a link.
Shumpton Mikolofskin invited me to his **event A Table Brother and Shane Oldman at Usual's Nooks and Feathers.**
Jess Onion shared his event with you: **Open-faced Noon: Scenery Silent from Bill Quarter and Lenny Ace.**
Did I know Eileen Varastus?

Hoosan Orly added a new photo.
Principal Laundryjuice was at Joint, Utah.
Molotov Wee Churchingness updated his status.
Wen Jivoltree commented on **Quisty Ainge's** photo.
Manual Polis invited me to **Sea Refusal.**
Barley Drick updated his status.
Did I know Mistard Hizzly?
Did I know Zebra Flowshot?
Piston McEenson also commented on **Eunice Perch's** status.
Houston Perch liked my comment: "Epistolary handprint—
   onerous number..."
One Day Porch invited me to like his rock **Kazoo.**
Weff Ropplon invited me to like Weff Ropplon.
Love Lonny invited me to like his page **Your Bones Aren't Me.**
Did I know Legg Jibb?
Shoepile Rotors liked my comment "Your naps!"
Shishpile Rotors posted on my Skinline.
Rushton Rotors liked a photo I am buried with.

The Rose of Maine

If love weren't so
Enormous I would live with its two hands
On me forever lifted.

Where else could silence bed
With adoration
Like a color spreading down a coast?

It's true what life does
Across a desk, what next week is,
How days kiss, and people get wet.

I'm organizing
Seed head-on. Skin
And then life

Builds from its chowder
Of questions on the street:
Whose blue

Billiard ball is this
So far from its table?
Whose can,
Emptied?

I Was Trying

I was trying (not) to get discouraged,
but the time was too tight.
First I dropped a penny
into the orange juice.
I was a fighter, fighting
(never) with the way I looked.

In the end, the beginning
came back around
the arm of the shed
and whacked me,
like the first thought
ever had.

Then it was time
to kiss,
and I kissed my own hand
by mistake, instead of hers.

The night knew all else
there was
to think (another word?),

and the same
things happened
at least twice, I know.

No big deal, the sun said,
realizing it was more
than just a circle.

And the thing I tell you
and you listen to it
way in and way out,

like there are ways
for us to reach
and pull a dollar down.

No bother, no matter,
great as this poem pulling me
through the halls of other people's

Hearts? Would we say that?
I (just) did, it says here.

And the room is rising to meet
the word it
signifies. I watch the rain
not know that it's water.

All the other times crowd around
to watch this one
climb up the pole,
that's the great way
life's taking it.

But taking what,
roughly, or exactly?

I couldn't know. Not
to worry (though),
the hill bursts out,
and then sleep,
and then later more water.

False Memory

Remember the day you were supposed to be at work
And you were still in New York?

I would say it was a 51 to 49 decision
And depending on the day
I was 51 and you were 49.

A Saturday: your head turns
And you don't mind much where you're from,
Bread baked the same way since 1930.

I used to live in the city
Where I could smell the nice, fresh bread.

I dropped a chesspiece and you fell.
And look, there was a red tree for a month,
The guy onstage when others think
They see the sun--he points off in a different direction and says
"That's where it will rise."

I woke up thinking we would do what we've never done.
I loved you because I had time.
It won't take two hours for friends to make.
The horns go off, in a large, unhurried way.

From chambered muscle to the seat of liking,
An arm of trees swings with the same new thoughts.
Talk thunders through the forest like a beautiful mate.
Meat of the illusionless, light held on, wind spread.

Galatea

He
misses narrating cheap Galatea's fossil
immortal of the Act, a beautiful John,
and his cyclops Poliferno insidious of
the day and sues voltage immortal of the
Finito, a glorious avarice and has his
voltage certainly attracted with his sin,
of his flute (symbolizing want). No essence
reuses nil his intent, suppressing the
body of love, scagging infuriating an
enormous mass cheating
Ragu, unintentionally, Acting. How
Raccoons nullify Metamorphoses' Ovid,
Galatea, by taking in life his love's
amour, transforming his blood in
the acto of surging in his
divine stress a day fluvius. It grabs
mythology has dates lunging all
diffusing in a soggy iconographic
predicament daily artistic of the
Renaissance, quelling the Triumph
of Galatea, if trying in a
vivacious scene and effluvia, never
quelling the ninja countrified at the

center, if stepping from a scene,
soul of the square, a couch trained
the definite. His group swerves
in the alcoves loving Che scagging freshness
in the direction of Galatea.

Central

A hotdog is not a sandwich,
water is not a ladder,
dragon piano removal is not the zebra on the highway.

A hotdog is not a dog,
kangaroos are not bridges for animals to cross,
windshield wipers are not blinkers.

Yuen is not chorizo sausage stacks,
the first page of a novel is not the only page,
a deaf driver is not a phlebotomist.

The water's boiling down is not time hurry up and pass,
a stingless bee is not Karen by the door,
a treeful of sulphur-crested cockatoos is not dream
        interpretation.

Epiphanies aren't all biblical, a small haphazard farm is not
pick your time. Getting here in two days is not
getting here in one, staying at the Hilton

at BWI on the first night is not sleeping on the plane,
the cancelled flight is not the only flight, the new flight
is not the one flight, two flights are not sleeves of pre-departure.

I'm glad is not firing salt into clouds,
tweeting shade is not 97% humidity!
The monkey of fish is not the burramundi.

Finally, here is not because our eyes are small,
the truck is not silver no it's silver but not gray,
are you sitting in a chair without arms is not

what is your favorite.
Olive my heart is not go ahead, I'm listening,
I have to go to high school is not the lipstick matches the flowers

on the tree behind her.

Fried Eggs on Night

for Ed Barrett

Whether nerves make souls shake
I'm here from coffee
Doesn't matter whether to reach in someone
Says soulfully, someone says,
If I cry I won't look at the map.
Physical and with the Celtics heating up
A memory where the sun's like dinner
It's pretty unusual today's worth at the sight of college.

In the alley that night Peter hugged us hanging onto us
While Jack was on his cell.
There's an element of the clock now starting to come up
But we're almost never over.
I can feel something not starting to bother me
Like lunch at Lubitsch with Lisa and Jim.

How not to think success fame or power
We were all in the boats twice once in spring
With Natalie when it was cold from seeming so.
I took the bus out to Schlossplatz to see the wrecking balls
The towers the only thing left

Laughed at Giant with the blonde woman who became a
    manager
Who gave me the funny recipe for lasagna.

I think of crossing at the corner we look for the right windows
In the middle of life
I see three things
The cardinal
Stands there without being afraid
I thought Natalie was lost
But she came out of the shop next door
Then we had lunch like we always do.

All tomorrow if you want fresh speech
A sliver of best moves, thank us to the end.
Who can love the air closing bell
Still leading the homes this past year connect the water
What is it the president said we're not afraid of
Breathing in wondering what the car is going to do it will let me off
Following news into last and later week yes I will
And those wild trees weeds without any real place
As the water feels like putting something in your mouth's hand
When the car door shuts and you hear it over interesting
That's tomorrow when the chicken should have been cooked
The index card left next to the phone
Not description for the hell of it

I'm Glad When You Rest

I'm glad when you rest, it's like you lived here,
And you see me from the convenience store and
My brains make you out.
It's like your ears had slid off
And like a picture had visited your forehead.
My heart has a face,
Then everyone knows everyone's
Changed the terms.
Fish-centered from now on.
Go farther than out in the ocean the open
And keep
"which I thought,"
One woman's words.
A turtle died here
But the boy didn't cry.
To prevent dead coals at spots.
My notes are missing I think I
Put them in a bag or in a suitcase.
Part of the reason for lakes is
Who'll forget what you liked to think about.
Found what worried you.

Please

Reflected three birds fly across the glass (reflected off the glass).
Please say if there's a problem with this poem
Report a problem with this poem

Elizabeth

The eye is looking for a thing, like a pine,
yes, a pine, with similar things around.
Pines complete the picture, along with a pizza
sign, a cement sign, and a real sign. Come in,
the mouth opens to say, even before the bell stops ringing.
An empty glass, from France, dries in the cloudy room.
The trusted room. Relax, the dust says, the eye sparkles
but can't invent. All of what is in this life
is in this room, the place itself hides no actions
and holds even less. And the pines, like kids'
voices in another yard, have experience
which the eye follows. More signs appear, and the glass dries.

The Nice Woman Phones

The nice woman phones the small man.

The little sister knows the ugly man.

The loud man visits the small mother.

The large boy buys the pretty picture.

The nice, beautiful woman eats the hot noodles.

The loud teacher drinks cold cola.

The nice woman knows the ugly man.

The rich man visits the loud mother.

The beautiful woman eats the hot noodles.

The nice teacher drinks cold cola.

Ruby Red

Clouds are going in right now
fitted for Boston or
to answer for all the United States.

For every month, there are only two days
when nothing can be done.
Today is the right day to mostly live.

In Dublin, New Hampshire
I might have smoked
over a new and improved plan.

However it's by our words
we would be judged,
right? Right Terence? Accuracy

and entertainment. Two
Sundays ago, we saw a cow
give birth to a calf.

We were just standing there
listening to this guy speak,
talk us through, and then the vet

and her helpers pulled,
and presto--vita nuova!
The ones who promote a

farming lifestyle.
And then footsteps, two pairs,
down the stairs,

and a walk is maybe due. Joy's
painted in stripes.
I asked someone today what

color is your hair and they
said, without pause,
ruby red.

A bell sound is nice but
you have to wonder
if it's really a bell.

But it's nice, the air
says, like a free book
on healing.

Summer wasn't cooler
but less nervous
southward, near to us.

All the Sudden

All the sudden, the tree stands there, like a synonym (for...)
The awful Mao Zedong once wrote, in a line when he's on his
        horse,
"The sky is three feet away."
Because I was watching *Gates of Eternity,*
because I was watching *Eternity's Gate,*
the whisper spot is again broken this year,
a word thing, meeting Elvis's commanding officer,
blind from the heat of the stove,
a spin along Bottle Alley.
I smell bread in heaven. I knew that today would come,
how worms see the color blue. Sometimes the world map
seems bigger than the earth itself.
Look at the sun on these cows, crows the size of dogs.
Consciousness starts with
a cute husky out there on the balcony.
He's always out there with a woman.
He's under the table.
The moose takes up only a quarter of its poem.
The heart of all this collectively fills even further,
a window with a feeling attached.
Crowds flood Bears Ears.
Something else: "Have some friends but not too many,"
the doctor said. Is that good? How many

should someone have?
Oh and a sprig of boxwood steeped in holy water,
sugared almonds for baptisms.
Blue Georgia save us.

Promising, New

The most beautiful photos that you send to us
Sit next to me like ships
That sail directly into the past, you know?
And everywhere there's music,
The world without clouds, button that I
Can press so lightly, in order to see everything.
Why did life decide
To begin and how many songs
Are there, approximately? You and you
Feel to me like metaphor that's the thing
Itself. Understand? Peter Altenberg
Is a new discovery, my poems
Will get shorter and shorter soon
With pleasure. Life reaches so far, how someone
Can see the asphalt, still pearls.
Your books please you, your rooms
Appear additionally
Toward the sun, Right? Like wood-roasted
Olives and Angie's lemon potatoes appear
The days, one after the other, singly, in a
Stream. "Hitch our worries to a horse and
Watch it glide." Little is still better than
A lot, the bookseller has ordered
Your books! My work is nothing to

Solve, everything to look at the rest
Of human life. No hurry to reach
The memories. I feel beauty
Suddenly, the bathwater is a little
Warmer, felt at the source.

Hamburger Theory

I will never think of you as dead even when you aren't
Dead anymore. The snow is up to my hips in the poem
I'd write about you. Honest,
I'm afraid to use the word day before it appears
Fifty times in the last poems
Written over the year.

I didn't write
For the masses right away.
It took more time.
I didn't do it right.
The plays that came sprayed with life,
The eyes that loved them but didn't see.

Ambiguity is good. Everything lousy
Isn't lousy for a reason, the phone
Still ringing after someone answers,
February, the home of eye contact.
She's tired, falls asleep,
He loves her, doesn't wake her.

Do you think our German will
Do something to itself long enough.
I think it's called

Having a thin neck.
Once my listening
Comprehension bites

The opportunity
To release tension,
Barbara puts her car
In a place where I could hit it
If I wanted to,
That I might finish this book.

A Letter

I hope, I pray,
smooth bark on four full moons,
a headstream
to live in the eyes,

a loop of colors
pours over the small part
of something,
if that's what you want to call it,
but call it I have.

It's really nice
remembering the sun,
and yes it's not everyday
a person says
"I'm the answer
to the question
that's never been asked."

So there's that, and then
this morning
and the night before that:
the plants I grew from seed
still hadn't shown,

like they're listening
for something.
It's like
waiting for glass to cool, no,

that's not it.
I lost MacBeth, plus
a notebook, on the plane.
They Fed-Exed them back
the next day.
I walked

up a hill
called Brewers Hill.
I went in Saint Casmir's
whose kids were playing
under the cherry flowers.

I wondered
were the Ways of the Cross
carved from wood,
was the baptismal
stone, did the women

really scrub the marble
steps?
I don't know what happens

like munj
enters rope.

Enough thought like
vines loving water,
the semi-necessary
not too diffident pen.
My wooden ruler.

Who knows where the sound
is coming from.
You turned your head
to see a book,
you stretched your arm

to pick it up
and opened it
and read,
turning the pages.
Sometimes, thoughts lead us

to the main hall or central room.
Time goes easy on us.
I thought I was sleeping,
rowing to London, um,
to tell someone.

To look at the way
and decide.
"Today is today"
is what Lisa said,
these first few hundred weeks.

A third of the fresh
water flowing into the
Mediterranean. The western coast's
alluvial, or terraced.
The eastern coast

is highly indented.
The sea
is relatively smooth.
Its bright green color
is a result of...

I forget.
The happier world
of headlamps,
the House of Curls.
I pray.

Please tell me
you're going to build a fountain.

When was the last time
you saw the ocean?
Tell me about that.

*

There was no way to tell whether what
I'd write would mean anything, to sleep
with my soul on, I don't remember
a lot but it was tremendous and
still seems like it, the sunlight and trees
not begging for description, time not
worried about where wind comes from, yes
to a hundred per cent not ninety
nine point nine anymore. I love
how they told you how long to keep your
teabag in, that when you write enough
Break off the first branch that brushes against
your hat on your way home and bring it
to me – the legend of the ones
who couldn't stop laughing. Don't forget loose,
the word that means close to your tongue, don't
feel like you have to be saying something.

Selected Poetry Titles Published by SurVision Books

Contemporary Tangential Surrealist Poetry: An Anthology
Edited by Tony Kitt
ISBN 978-1-912963-44-7

Invasion: An Anthology of Ukrainian Poetry about the War
Edited by Tony Kitt
ISBN 978-1-912963-32-4

Noelle Kocot. *Humanity*
(New Poetics: USA)
ISBN 978-1-9995903-0-7

Marc Vincenz. *Visitation*
(New Poetics: USA)
ISBN 978-1-912963-48-5

Helen Ivory. *Maps of the Abandoned City*
(New Poetics: England)
ISBN 978-1-912963-04-1

Tony Kitt. *The Magic Phlute*
(New Poetics: Ireland)
ISBN 978-1-912963-08-9

John Bradley. *Spontaneous Mummification*
(Winner of James Tate Poetry Prize 2019)
ISBN 978-1-912963-13-3

Charles Borkhuis. *Spontaneous Combustion*
(Winner of James Tate Poetry Prize 2021)
ISBN 978-1-912963-30-0

Order our books from http://survisionmagazine.com